# The Concise Illustrated Book of
# Fighters of World War II

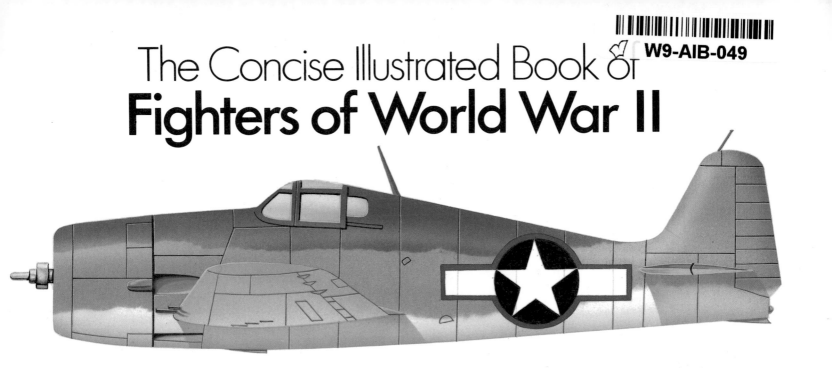

## Edited by D. Avery

GALLERY BOOKS
An imprint of W. H. Smith Publishers Inc.
112 Madison Avenue
New York, New York 10016

First published in the United States of
America by GALLERY BOOKS
An imprint of W. H. Smith Publishers Inc.
112 Madison Avenue
New York, New York 10016

ISBN 0-8317-9663-4

Printed in the German Democratic
Republic

**Acknowledgments**
All photographs from BTPH except:
Aviation Photographs International/J.
Flack 14, 16, 19, 27, 28, 35, 45; G.
Burridge 6; N. Burridge front cover, title
page, 7; H. W. Cowin 21, 23, 37; Novosti
Press Agency 29, 38; RAF Museum 11, 15,
20, 24, 25, 33, 34, 41, 42, 44, 46; TRH
Pictures 22, 30, 39, 43.

All artworks supplied by Maltings
Partnership except:
Andrew Wright 20, 27.

*A preserved flying example of a P-51
Mustang seen here at North Weald,
Essex, England in 1988.*

# CONTENTS

# BELL P-39 AIRACOBRA

This unconventional fighter was designed by R. J. Woods as the Bell Model 12. Its layout placed its large 37mm cannon in the nose firing through the propeller hub, and thus along the aircraft's centre line. This was achieved by installing the engine just behind the cockpit, and driving the propeller via a long shaft which ran under the pilot's seat. It entered service in 1939, and 9,589 were eventually manufactured.

*The Confederate Air Force's P-39 on display at their annual airshow at Harlingen, Texas.*

**Country of Origin:** United States
**Type:** fighter
**Crew:** one
**Power Plant:** one 1,200hp Allison V-1710-35 liquid-cooled vee-twelve mounted aft of the cockpit driving a tractor propeller by means of a long extension shaft
**Dimensions:** span 10.4m (34ft); length 9.2m (30ft 2in); height 3.7m (12ft 5in); wing area 19.8m² (213sq ft)
**Weights:** empty 2,561kg (5,645lb); loaded 3,765kg (8,300lb)
**Performance:** maximum speed 539km/h (335mph); service ceiling 10,670m (35,000ft); range 1,046km (650 miles)
**Armament:** one 37mm cannon firing through the propeller hub, two 0.5in machine-guns firing through the propeller arc, four 0.303in machine-guns in the wings, plus provision for one 227kg (500lb) bomb

# BELL P-63 KINGCOBRA

Developed from the P-39 Airacobra, the Kingcobra had a newly designed laminar-flow wing and increased power provided by its mid-mounted Allison engine driving a four-bladed propeller, together with revised tail surfaces. Of 3,303 P-63s built, most were sent to the Soviet Union under the Lend-Lease Agreement, the Free French Air Force receiving 300.

*A P-63 Kingcobra in Soviet colours at the North Weald Fighter Meet, 1988.*

**Country of Origin:** United States
**Type:** fighter
**Crew:** one
**Power Plant:** one 1,325hp Allison V-1710-95 liquid-cooled vee-twelve mounted aft of the cockpit driving a tractor propeller via long extension shaft
**Dimensions:** span 11.68m (38ft 4in); length 9.96m (32ft 8in); height 3.84m (12ft 7in)
**Weights:** empty 2,892kg (6,375lb); loaded 3,992kg (8,800lb)
**Performance:** maximum speed 657km/h (408mph); service ceiling 13,105m (43,000ft); range 724km (450 miles)
**Armament:** one 37mm cannon firing through the propeller hub; two 0.5in machine-guns firing through the propeller arc plus one in each wing; provision for one 227kg (500lb) bomb beneath the fuselage and two under the wings

# BOULTON PAUL DEFIANT MkI

Designed to meet Air Ministry Specification F.9/35, the Defiant's only armament was mounted in the power-operated turret located behind the cockpit. The first flight in August 1937 was followed by an initial order of 87 aircraft for the Royal Air Force. A total of 1,064 Defiants were built, most serving as night fighters in their all-over matt black finish and with new airborne radar.

**Country of Origin:** Great Britain
**Type:** fighter
**Crew:** two
**Power Plant:** one 1,030hp Rolls-Royce Merlin III liquid-cooled vee-twelve
**Dimensions:** span 12m (39ft 4in); length 10.8m (35ft 4in); height 3.7m (12ft 2in)
**Weights:** empty 2,756kg (6,078lb); loaded 3,900kg (8,600lb)
**Performance:** maximum speed 489km/h (304mph); service ceiling 9,250m (30,350ft); range 748km (465 miles)
**Armament:** four 0.303in Browning machine-guns in dorsal turret

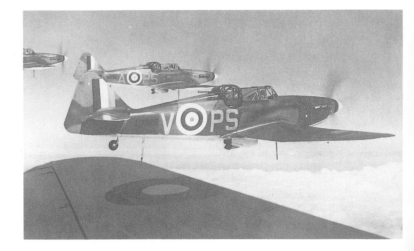

*The retractable radio masts are shown extended downwards on the aircraft in this flight of Defiants from 264 Sqn in March 1940.*

The XF2A-1 Buffalo made its maiden flight in January 1938, but despite being the US Navy's first monoplane fighter saw little success with that service. It was also ordered by Belgium, Britain and Finland, the Finnish Buffaloes remaining in front-line service until mid-1944.

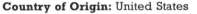

**Country of Origin:** United States
**Type:** fighter
**Crew:** one
**Power Plant:** one 940hp Wright R-1820-34 Cyclone 9-cylinder single-row air-cooled radial
**Dimensions:** span 10.67m (35ft); length 8.03m (26ft 4in); height 3.68m (12ft 1in)
**Weights:** empty 2,100kg (4,630lb); loaded 3,200kg (7,055lb)
**Performance:** maximum speed 484km/h (301mph); service ceiling 9,906m (32,500ft); range 1,762km (1,095 miles)
**Armament:** two 0.5in Colt-Browning machine-guns in upper engine cowling firing through propeller arc, and two in the wings

*The XF2A-2, an improved version of the original Buffalo, ordered by the US Navy, with a more powerful engine and flotation gear.*

# BRISTOL BEAUFIGHTER Mk1

The private venture prototype Beaufighter first flew on 17 July 1939. Its design was based on the Bristol Beaufort torpedo bomber utilizing its wings, tail-unit and rear fuselage. In service the Beaufighter proved to be an excellent night fighter with its airborne radar and heavy armament. Mk II Beaufighters were produced with a 1,280hp Rolls-Royce Merlin in place of the Hercules.

**Country of Origin:** Great Britain
**Type:** night fighter
**Crew:** two
**Power Plant:** two 1,600hp Bristol Hercules VI 14-cylinder two-row air-cooled sleeve-valve radials
**Dimensions:** span 17.6m (57ft 10in); length 12.6m (41ft 4in); height 4.8m (15ft 10in); wing area 46.7m$^2$ (503sq ft)
**Weights:** empty 6,380kg (14,070lb); loaded 9,435kg (20,800lb)
**Performance:** maximum speed 530km/h (330mph); service ceiling 8,840m (29,000ft); range 2,410km (1,498 miles)
**Armament:** four 20mm cannon in belly; two 0.303in Browning machine-guns in the port wing and four in the starboard wing; provision for eight 7.5cm (3in) rockets on wing rails; one 728kg (1,605lb) torpedo; or up to 450kg (1,000lb) of bombs

*A Beaufighter showing the dihedralled tailplane fitted to later models to improve directional stability primarily on take-off.*

1934 saw the appearance of the Bristol 142, a six to seven seat fast executive transport designed at the request of Lord Rothermere. This airplane had a very impressive performance which did not escape the attention of the military, and in Air Ministry tests the airplane reached speeds much faster than the RAF fighters of the day. As a result the Blenheim bomber was developed, with a new fuselage to accommodate a bomb bay. Many of these Blenheims were converted later to Blenheim IF fighter standard.

**Country of Origin:** Great Britain
**Type:** fighter
**Crew:** three
**Power Plant:** two 920hp Bristol Mercury XV air-cooled radials
**Dimensions:** span 17.17m (56ft 4in); length 13m (42ft 9in); height 3.66m (12ft)
**Weights:** empty 4,441kg (9,790lb); loaded 6,545kg (14,429lb)
**Performance:** maximum speed 402km/h (250mph); service ceiling 9,600m (31,500ft); range 3,138km (1,950 miles)
**Armament:** four fixed 0.303in Browning machine-guns in pod under fuselage; plus two in the dorsal turret

*A Mk 1F Blenheim of 90 Sqn Royal Air Force.*

# COMMONWEALTH BOOMERANG

This was designed as a stop-gap fighter for the Royal Australian Air Force after the Japanese attacked the American Pacific port of Pearl Harbor on 7 December 1941. Based on Commonwealth's Wirraway general purpose aircraft, the prototype Boomerang designated CA-12 first flew on 29 May 1941.

**Country of Origin:** Australia
**Type:** fighter
**Crew:** one
**Power Plant:** one 1,200hp Pratt & Whitney R-1830 Twin Wasp 14-cylinder two-row air-cooled radial
**Dimensions:** span 11.04m (36ft 3in); length 7.77m (25ft 6in); height 3.5m (11ft 6in)
**Weights:** empty 2,472kg (5,450lb); loaded 3,450kg (7,600lb)
**Performance:** maximum speed 476km/h (296mph); service ceiling 8,839m (29,000ft); range 1,496km (930 miles)
**Armament:** two 20mm Hispano cannon, and four 0.303in Browning machine-guns in the wings

*A Royal Australian Air Force Boomerang being guided from its jungle clearing by ground handlers.*

# CURTISS P-36 MOHAWK

France ordered large numbers of the P-36 for the French Armée de l'Air, as the Hawk 75A. Those that were delivered before the fall of France saw service against the Luftwaffe in May 1940, and shot down more than 300 German aircraft. The remainder of them were passed on to the Royal Air Force, entering service as Mohawks, and mainly saw action in Burma.

**Country of Origin:** United States
**Type:** fighter
**Crew:** one
**Power Plant:** 1,050hp Pratt & Whitney R-1830 Twin Wasp two-row air-cooled radial
**Dimensions:** span 11.36m (37ft 3½in); length 8.7m (28ft 7in); height 2.89m (9ft 6in)
**Weights:** empty 2.060kg (4,541lb); loaded 3,022kg (6,662lb)
**Performance:** maximum speed 488km/h (303mph); service ceiling 9,144m (30,000ft); range 1,094km (680 miles) on internal fuel
**Armament:** (P-36C) one 0.50in and one 0.30in Browning machine-gun above engine, plus two 0.30in machine-guns in wings, provision for 181kg (400lb) of bombs on underwing racks

*A P-36 of the US Army Air Corps painted in a multi-tone camouflage for a 1938 army exercise.*

# CURTISS P-40 HAWKS
## (C) P-40C TOMAHAWK,
## (N) P-40N KITTYHAWK IV

The first flight of the prototype XP-40, a converted P-36A, was in October 1938. The RAF's first P-40s were machines that had been ordered by the Armée de l'Air but diverted after France's capitulation, before finally entering service as the Tomahawk I. Poor armament meant they were used only for army co-operation purposes or sent out to the Far East.

*The Old Flying Machine Company's preserved P-40 Kittyhawk.*

**Country of Origin:** United States
**Type:** pursuit, reconnaissance, fighter-bomber and ground-attack
**Crew:** one
**Power Plant:** (C) one 1,040hp Allison V-1710-33, (N) one 1,200hp Allison, both liquid-cooled vee-twelves
**Dimensions:** span 11.36m (37ft 3½in); length (C) 9.7m (31ft 8½in), (N) 10.16m (33ft 4in); height 3.75m (12ft 4in)
**Weights:** empty (C) 2,636kg (5,812lb), (N) 3,039kg (6,700lb); loaded (C) 3,383kg (7,459lb), (N) 5,171kg (11,400lb)
**Performance:** maximum speed (C) 555km/h (345mph), (N) 552km/h (343mph); service ceiling 9,144m (30,000ft); range (C) 1,175km (730 miles), (N) 1,207km (750 miles)
**Armament:** (C) two 0.303in machine-guns in top of engine cowling, plus four mounted in the wings, (N) six 0.50in machine guns in wings, (N) one 272kg (600lb) bomb on centreline and one 227kg (500lb) bomb under each wing

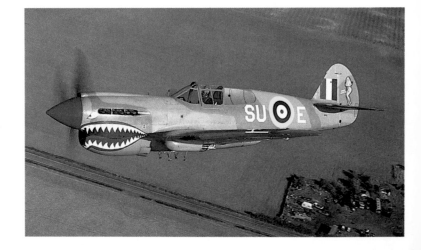

The first flight of the DH 98 was on 25 November 1940. Built almost entirely of wood, and nicknamed 'The Wooden Wonder', it was originally conceived as a fast day bomber. However, it was to prove so successful in every theatre it served in, and in every role that it played, that it soon became a legend among its pilots, and sought after by all Commands of the RAF. Night fighter variants carried airborne interception radar in the nose.

**Country of Origin:** Great Britain
**Type:** night fighter, photo-reconnaissance, bomber
**Crew:** two
**Power Plant:** two 1,460hp Rolls-Royce Merlin 21/23 liquid-cooled vee-twelves
**Dimensions:** span 16.5m (54ft 2in); length 13.6m (44ft 6in); height 5.03m (16ft 6in); wing area 42.2m² (454sq ft)
**Weights:** empty 6,638kg (14,635lb); loaded 10,430kg (23,000lb)
**Performance:** maximum speed 656km/h (408mph); service ceiling 11,278m (37,000ft); range 2,390km (1,485 miles)
**Armament:** (night fighter) four 20mm Hispano cannon in belly plus four 0.303in Browning machine-guns in the nose; (bomber variants) max bomb load 1,810kg (4,000lb)

*A Mosquito Mk IV of 143 Sqn at Banff being loaded with eight 27kg (60lb) rocket projectiles.*

# DEWOITINE D.520

First flight of the Dewoitine D.520 designed by Robert Castello was on 2 October 1938. Initial production was slow and only 36 aircraft were in service with the Armée de l'Air when the German offensive against France commenced. Production continued under France's Vichy government, and the Luftwaffe also flew them.

**Country of Origin:** France
**Type:** fighter
**Crew:** one
**Power Plant:** one 930hp Hispano-Suiza 12Y-45 liquid-cooled vee-twelve
**Dimensions:** span 10.2m (33ft 6in); length 8.76m (28ft 9in); height 2.57m (8ft 5in)
**Weights:** empty 2,100kg (4,630lb); loaded 2,800kg (6,173lb)
**Performance:** maximum speed 525km/h (326mph); service ceiling 11,000m (36,090ft); range 990km (615 miles)
**Armament:** one 20mm Hispano HS 404 cannon firing through the propeller hub, plus two 7.5mm MAC 1934-M39 machine-guns in each wing

*The Musée de l'Air's preserved D.520 at Le Bourget, Paris, France.*

# FIAT G.50 FRECCIA

This was designed by Ing. Giuseppe Gabrielli, to meet a specification issued by the Regia Aeronautica in 1935 for an all-metal monoplane fighter for the Italian Air Force. Forty-five G.50s were initially ordered from a Fiat subsidiary CMASA, and deliveries began in January 1938. This aircraft served in Europe, the Mediterranean and North Africa.

**Country of Origin:** Italy
**Type:** fighter, fighter-bomber
**Crew:** one
**Power Plant:** one 840hp Fiat A.74 RC38 14-cylinder two-row air-cooled radial
**Dimensions:** span 10.9m (36ft 1in); length 7.8m (25ft 7in); height 2.97m (9ft 9in); wing area 18.25m² (196sq ft)
**Weights:** empty 2,015kg (4,443lb); loaded 2,522kg (5,560lb)
**Performance:** maximum speed 470km/h (293mph); service ceiling 10,700m (35,106ft); range 676km (420 miles)
**Armament:** two 12.7mm Breda-SAFAT machine-guns in fuselage; provision for 300kg (660lb) bombs

*Extremely under-armed and armoured, the Fiat G.50 proved inferior to most of its opponents.*

# FOCKE WULF Fw-190

On 1 June 1939, three months before WWII started, the FW 190V-1 prototype, which had been designed by Kurt Tank, made its first flight. It remained unknown to the allies until first encountered over France early in 1941, and immediately proved itself to be far superior to the Spitfire V then in RAF service. Later versions were powered by a 12-cylinder Junkers Jumo vee-twelve.

**Country of Origin:** Germany
**Type:** fighter
**Crew:** one
**Power Plant:** one 1,700hp (2,100hp with emergency boost) BMW 801D 18-cylinder two-row air-cooled radial
**Dimensions:** span 10.5m (34ft 6in); length 8.84m (29ft); height 3.96m (13ft); wing area 18.2m² (196sq ft)
**Weights:** empty 3,471kg (7,652lb); loaded 4,900kg (10,802lb)
**Performance:** maximum speed 650–675km/h (404–419mph); service ceiling 11,400m (37,400ft); range 900km (560 miles)
**Armament:** two 13mm MG131 machine-guns in upper engine cowling, two 20mm MG151 cannon in wing roots plus two outboard

*An Fw-190 'Dora-9' of JG 3 'Udet'. This variant was affectionately dubbed 'Langnasen Dora' by its crews.*

# GLOSTER GLADIATOR

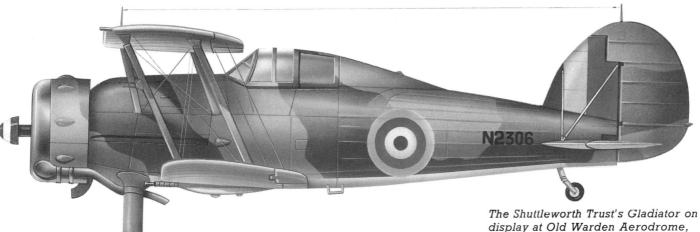

*The Shuttleworth Trust's Gladiator on display at Old Warden Aerodrome, Biggleswade, England.*

First flight of the private venture S.S.37 was in September 1934, and following RAF evaluation in April 1935 the aeroplane was put into production as the Gladiator Mk 1, differing from the S.S.37 in having a more powerful engine and an enclosed cockpit. The Gladiator was the last biplane fighter to see service in the RAF. It was three of these outmoded fighters which helped to defend Malta against far superior enemy forces and in doing so to help win for the island the George Cross. The Sea Gladiator was a variant flown by the Fleet Air Arm.

**Country of Origin:** Great Britain
**Type:** fighter
**Crew:** one
**Power Plant:** one 840hp Bristol Mercury VIIIA 9-cylinder air-cooled radial
**Dimensions:** span 9.8m (32ft 3in); length 8.4m (27ft 5in); height 3.6m (11ft 9in); wing area 30m² (323sq ft)
**Weights:** empty 1,565kg (3,450lb); loaded 2,155kg (4,750lb)
**Performance:** maximum speed 414km/h (257mph); service ceiling 10,210m (33,500ft); range 690–710km (430–440 miles)
**Armament:** four 0.303in Browning machine-guns, two mounted in forward fuselage and two in pods under wings

# GLOSTER METEOR I

This was the only allied jet fighter to see service in WWII. Designed by George Carter to meet Air Ministry Specification F.9/40, the prototype Meteor first flew on 5 March 1943. Production aircraft were delivered to No. 616 Sqn of the RAF in July 1944, and saw service in August of the same year, being deployed against Germany's high speed, unmanned V-1 Flying Bomb over southern England, this being the only jet-jet combat of WWII.

**Country of Origin:** Great Britain
**Type:** fighter
**Crew:** one
**Power Plant:** two 770kg (1,700lb) thrust Rolls-Royce W.2B/23C Welland series 1 turbojets
**Dimensions:** span 13.1m (43ft); length 12.6m (41ft 3in); height 3.96m (13ft); wing area 34.7m² (374sq ft)
**Weights:** empty 3,690kg (8,140lb); loaded 6,260kg (13,800lb)
**Performance:** maximum speed 668km/h (415mph); service ceiling 12,190m (40,000ft); range approximately 1,610km (1,000 miles)
**Armament:** four 20mm British Hispano cannon in front fuselage

*A Mk F III Meteor of 616 Sqn RAF in Germany in April 1945.*

# GRUMMAN F4F WILDCAT

This carrier-based aircraft entered service in 1940 with the Fleet Air Arm as Martlet Is and with the US Navy. They were particularly effective flying from aircraft carriers in the Pacific battles of the Coral Sea and Midway.

**Country of Origin:** United States
**Type:** naval fighter
**Crew:** one
**Power Plant:** one 1,200hp Pratt & Whitney Twin Wasp R-1830-86 14-cylinder two-row air-cooled radial
**Dimensions:** span 11.6m (38ft); length 8.8m (28ft 9in); height 3.6m (11ft 10in); wing area 24.2m² (260sq ft)
**Weights:** empty 2,109kg (4,649lb); loaded 2,767kg (6,100lb)
**Performance:** maximum speed 531km/h (330mph); service ceiling 8,534m (28,000ft); range 1,850km (1,150 miles)
**Armament:** six 0.5in machine-guns mounted in wings

*'The Wildcat, it is no exaggeration to say, did more than any single instrument of war to save the day for the US in the Pacific'*
*Foster Hailey, New York Times, 1943.*

# GRUMMAN F6F HELLCAT

It first flew on 26 June 1942 as the XF6F-1 with a 1,700hp Wright R-2600-10 Cyclone engine. Hellcat production began with the F6F-3 entering service with Britain's Fleet Air Arm in July 1943, and with the US Navy in August operating mainly in the Pacific.

**Country of Origin:** United States
**Type:** naval fighter
**Crew:** one
**Power Plant:** one 2,000hp Pratt & Whitney R-2800-10W Double Wasp 18-cylinder two-row air-cooled radial
**Dimensions:** span 13.1m (42ft 10in); length 10.2m (33ft 7in); height 4m (13ft 1in); wing area 31m² (334sq ft)
**Weights:** empty 4,179kg (9,212lb); loaded 6,240kg (13,758lb)
**Performance:** maximum speed 597km/h (371mph); service ceiling 11,190m (36,600ft); range 2,460km (1,530 miles)
**Armament:** six 0.5in machine-guns in wings; up to 907kg (2,000lb) of bombs, or six 3in rockets under wings

*The rugged Hellcat outgunned nearly every Japanese fighter in the Pacific. It was credited with 4,947 enemy planes destroyed.*

Sidney Camm's classic monoplane fighter design. Development work to replace the Fury biplane began as early as 1933 with the first flight on 6 November 1935. By the outbreak of war in September 1939, 497 had been delivered.

**Country of Origin:** Great Britain
**Type:** fighter
**Crew:** one
**Power Plant:** one 1,030hp Rolls-Royce Merlin II liquid-cooled vee-twelve
**Dimensions:** span 12.2m (40ft); length 9.5m (31ft 4in); height 4m (13ft 1in); wing area 24m² (259sq ft)
**Weights:** empty 2,151kg (4,743lb); loaded 2,820kg (6,218lb)
**Performance:** maximum speed 496km/h (308mph); service ceiling 10,180m (33,400ft); range 845km (525 miles)
**Armament:** eight 0.303in Browning machine-guns in wings; up to 454kg (1,000lb) bombs under wings

*The Battle of Britain Memorial Flight's Hurricane Mk IIC showing the RAF's unusual black/white underside of the early war years.*

23

# HAWKER TEMPEST (II, V AND VI)

Originally named the Typhoon II, the Tempest was designed to meet specification F.10/41, employing a newly designed laminar-flow wing section, to avoid some of the Typhoon's undesirable handling characteristics. It entered service in time to meet the threat of Hitler's flying bomb and accounted for over one-third of all V-1s shot down by RAF aircraft.

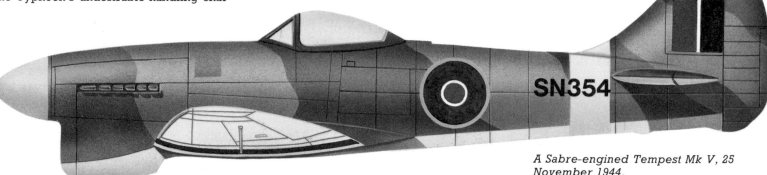

SN354

*A Sabre-engined Tempest Mk V, 25 November 1944.*

**Country of Origin:** Great Britain
**Type:** fighter-bomber
**Crew:** one
**Power Plant:** (II) one 2,526hp Bristol Centaurus 18-cylinder sleeve-valve two-row air-cooled radial, (V) one 2,180hp Napier Sabre IIA, B or C 24-cylinder sleeve-valve liquid-cooled flat "H", (VI) one 2,340hp Sabre V
**Dimensions:** span 12.5m (41ft); length (II) 10.5m (34ft 5in), (V, VI) 10.26m (33ft 8in); height (II) 4.8m (15ft 10in), (V, VI) 4.9m (16ft 1in)
**Weights:** empty (II) 4,037kg (8,900lb), (V, VI) 4,128kg (9,100lb); loaded (II) 6,010kg (13,250lb), (V, VI) 6,130kg (13,500lb)
**Performance:** maximum speed (II) 708km/h (440mph), (V) 688km/h (427mph), (VI) 704km/h (438mph); service ceiling 11,280m (37,000ft); range (II) 1,319km (820 miles), (V, VI) 1,191km (740 miles)
**Armament:** two 20mm Hispano Mk II cannon in each wing plus provision for two 454kg (1,000lb) bombs or eight 27kg (60lb) rocket projectiles beneath the wings

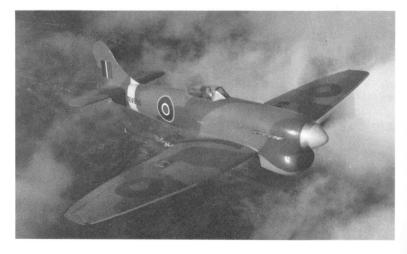

Hawker's design team led by Sidney Camm set to work to meet specification F.18/37 for an interceptor. Two new power plants were though suitable: the Rolls-Royce Vulture and the Napier Sabre. Two prototypes were constructed, but the Vulture-engined project, named Tornado, was curtailed when Rolls-Royce cancelled engine development, leaving the Typhoon to continue into service.

**Country of Origin:** Great Britain
**Type:** fighter-bomber
**Crew:** one
**Power Plant:** one 2,220hp Napier Sabre IIB 24-cylinder liquid-cooled sleeve-valve flat "H"
**Dimensions:** span 12.7m (41ft 7in); length 9.7m (31ft 11in); height 4.7m (15ft 4in); wing area 25.9m² (279sq ft)
**Weights:** empty 3,992kg (8,800lb); loaded 6,010kg (13,250lb)
**Performance:** maximum speed 663km/h (412mph); service ceiling 10,730m (35,200ft); range 820km (510 miles) on internal fuel with bombs, or 1,577km (980 miles) with drop tanks
**Armament:** four 20mm Hispano cannon; provision for eight 3in rocket projectiles or two 454kg (1,000lb) bombs

*A Typhoon Mk IB of 257 Sqn at Warmwell, England, in May 1943.*

# HEINKEL He 219 UHU

Ernst Heinkel's proposals for a high-speed fighter, bomber and torpedo bomber aroused little interest from the German authorities when he showed them his designs in 1940. However, when RAF night bombing raids began to take their toll on German industry, it was realised that the Luftwaffe needed a fast, radar-equipped night fighter. The He 219 Uhu ('Owl') was put into production following a first flight on 15 November 1942, and proved very effective even against the fast-flying Mosquitoes.

**Country of Origin:** Germany
**Type:** night fighter
**Crew:** two
**Power Plant:** two 1,800hp Daimler-Benz DB603E liquid-cooled inverted-vee-twelves
**Dimensions:** span 18.5m (60ft 8in); length 15.5m (50ft 10in); height 4.1m (13ft 5in); wing area 44.5m² (479sq ft)
**Weights:** empty 9,900kg (21,826lb); loaded 13,150kg (28,990lb)
**Performance:** maximum speed 630km/h (391mph); service ceiling 11,300m (37,070ft); range 2,800km (1,740 miles)
**Armament:** two 20mm MC151 cannon in wings; two 30mm MK108 in ventral tray; two oblique upward-firing 30mm MK108 cannon in rear fuselage

*A captured He 219 A-5 pictured here in RAF markings at Farnborough, England after the war.*

Developed as a night fighter from the Ju 88A bomber. Initial fighter variants, the Ju 88C series, entered service in late 1940, these aircraft having a revised nose containing machine-gun and cannon armament plus Lichtenstein radar. Early in 1944 the Ju 88G appeared. This had heavier armament, improved radar and a more square-cut fin and rudder as used on the Ju 188.

**Country of Origin:** Germany
**Type:** night fighter
**Crew:** three
**Power Plant:** two 1,880hp Junkers Jumo liquid-cooled 12-cylinder inverted-vee
**Dimensions:** span 20.08m (65ft 10½in); length 16.5m (54ft 1½in); height 4.85m (15ft 11in)
**Weights:** empty 9,100kg (20,062lb); loaded 14,674kg (32,350lb)
**Performance:** maximum speed 647km/h (402mph); service ceiling 8,800m (28,870ft); range 2,300km (1,430 miles)
**Armament:** four 20mm MG 151/20 firing forward from ventral fairing, two MG 151/20 in Schräge Musik installation plus one 13mm MG 131 in rear of cabin

*A Ju 88 on display at RAF St. Athan, still sporting the RAF serial number that was applied when it was captured.*

# LAVOCHKIN La-7

Entering service with the Soviet Air Force mid-way through 1944, the La-7 was an aerodynamically improved version of the La-5FN which had proved itself in combat against both the Fw 190A-4 and Bf 109G. The La-7 was probably the USSR's best wartime fighter.

**Country of Origin:** Soviet Union
**Type:** interceptor fighter
**Crew:** one
**Power Plant:** one 1,700hp Shvetsov M-82FN 14-cylinder two-row air-cooled radial
**Dimensions:** span 9.8m (32ft 2in); length 8.5m (27ft 11in); height 2.84m (9ft 3in); wing area 17.5m² (188.4sq ft)
**Weights:** empty 2,638kg (5,816lb); loaded 3,400kg (7,496lb)
**Performance:** maximum speed 680km/h (423mph); service ceiling 10,500m (34,450ft); range 635km (395 miles)
**Armament:** three 20mm ShVAK cannon in upper cowling; provision for 200kg (440lb) bombs or six RS-82 rockets on underwing racks

*Very much the product of hard-won combat experience, the La-7 went a long way to correcting the faults of the disappointing La-5.*

The maiden flight of the I-22 fighter was on 30 March 1939. Unconventionally for its day it was built almost entirely of wood. It went into production as the Lagg-1, but lacking the performance of other Soviet fighters, it was soon replaced by the more powerful Lagg-3 which also had leading-edge wing slats and improved armament.

**Country of Origin:** Soviet Union
**Type:** fighter
**Crew:** one
**Power Plant:** one 1,240hp M-105PF liquid-cooled vee-twelve
**Dimensions:** span 9.8m (32ft 2in); length 8.6m (28ft 1in); height 2.7m (8ft 10in); wing area 17.5m² (188.4sq ft)
**Weights:** empty 2,620kg (5,776lb); loaded 3,300kg (7,275lb)
**Performance:** maximum speed 560km/h (348mph); service ceiling 9,600m (31,500ft); range 650km (404 miles)
**Armament:** one 20mm ShVAK cannon firing through the propeller hub; two 12.7mm BS machine-guns in upper cowling; provision for 200kg (440lb) bomb load, or six 82mm RS 82 rocket projectiles

*Robustness of structure and clean lines characterized the Lagg-3, the Soviet's near contemporary of the Hawker Hurricane.*

# LOCKHEED P-38 LIGHTNING (J)

Lockheed's prototype long-range fighter, the XP-38, first flew on 27 January 1939, just 15 days later taking off from California and flying to New York in 7 hours, 2 minutes with two refuelling stops. It was however damaged beyond repair upon landing. Despite this, USAAC production began later in 1939. The P-38 was a highly successful long-range tactical fighter, and was flown in every theatre of war.

**Country of Origin:** United States
**Type:** long-range fighter
**Crew:** one
**Power Plant:** two 1,425hp Allison V-1710 liquid-cooled vee-twelves
**Dimensions:** span 15.85m (52ft); length 11.5m (37ft 10in); height 3m (9ft 10in); wing area 30.4m² (327sq ft)
**Weights:** empty 6,169kg (13,600lb); loaded 9,070kg (20,000lb)
**Performance:** maximum speed 666km/h (414mph); service ceiling 13,410m (44,000ft); range 1,891km (1,175 miles) on internal fuel
**Armament:** one 20mm Hispano cannon and four 0.5in Browning machine-guns in nose; maximum bomb load 907kg (2,000lb)

*The P-38F Lightning's turbochargers are visible on top of the booms just behind the wing's trailing edge and in front of the radiators.*

# MACCHI MC 200 SAETTA

Having cut their teeth on the Schneider racing seaplanes, Aeronautica Macchi's design team, led by Ing. Mario Castoldi, set about designing a monoplane fighter for the Regie Aeronautica, the Italian Air Force. The production aircraft's performance was limited by a low-powered engine, and the insistence of Italian pilots that the aircraft should have an open cockpit and a fixed tailwheel. It also had poor armament, but was very agile in dogfights.

**Country of Origin:** Italy
**Type:** interceptor fighter
**Crew:** one
**Power Plant:** one 870hp Fiat A.74 RC 38 14-cylinder two-row air-cooled radial
**Dimensions:** span 10.6m (34ft 8⅓in); length 8.2m (26ft 10½in); height 3.5m (11ft 6¼in); wing area 16.8m² (181sq ft)
**Weights:** empty 1,769kg (3,900lb); loaded 2,200kg (4,850lb)
**Performance:** maximum speed 502km/h (312mph); service ceiling 8,900m (29,200ft); range 870km (540 miles)
**Armament:** two 12.7mm Breda-SAFAT machine-guns in upper cowling with later models also having one 7.7mm machine-gun in each wing and provision for up to 160kg (352lb) of bombs on underwing racks

*Of antiquated appearance, the MC 200 nonetheless was very agile, readily bettering the Hurricane in one-to-one combat.*

# MACCHI MC 205 VELTRO

The poor performance of the Saetta led to the development of the C.202 Folgore with a much more powerful liquid-cooled Alfa-Romeo built (DB 601A-1) engine. This was later replaced by a Fiat-built DB 605A-1 in the C.205 Veltro which first flew on 19 April 1942.

**Country of Origin:** Italy
**Type:** fighter, fighter-bomber
**Crew:** one
**Power Plant:** one 1,475 Fiat RA.1050 RC 58 Tifone liquid-cooled inverted-vee-twelve
**Dimensions:** span 10.6m (34ft 8½in); length 8.85m (29ft ½in); height 3m (9ft 10½in); wing area 16.8m² (180.8sq ft)
**Weights:** empty 2,581kg (5,691lb); loaded 3,408kg (7,514lb)
**Performance:** maximum speed 642km/h (399mph); service ceiling 11,000m (36,090ft); range 1,040km (646 miles)
**Armament:** two 12.7mm Breda-SAFAT machine-guns in upper cowling; two 7.7mm Breda-SAFAT machine-guns in wings; maximum bomb load 318kg (700lb)

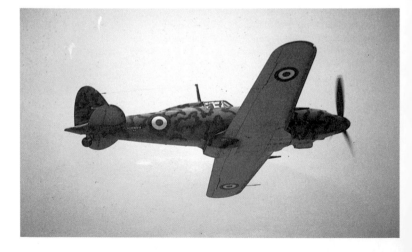

*Aermacchi's airworthy MC 205 Veltro at an Italian air display.*

32

# MESSERSCHMITT Bf 109 (E AND G)

Due to the unavailability of a suitable German engine, the first Bf 109 flew in September 1935, powered by a British-built Rolls-Royce Kestrel. Bf 109Es or 'Emils' were the Luftwaffe's main fighter throughout the Battle of Britain and until late 1942 when production switched to 109Fs and more importantly the 109G or 'Gustav' which was the last important production model.

*A Bf-109K with an Fw-190A behind. These two types fought over Germany against overwhelming odds in 1945 during daytime bombing raids by the USAAF.*

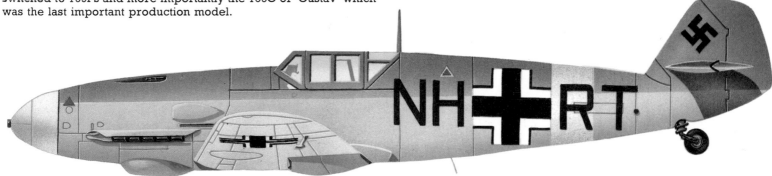

**Country of Origin:** Germany
**Type:** fighter
**Crew:** one
**Power Plant:** (E) one 1,300hp Daimler-Benz DB 601A, (G) one 1,475hp DB 605; both 12-cylinder liquid-cooled inverted-vees
**Dimensions:** span (E) 9.87m (32ft 4½in), (G) 9.9m (32ft 6½in); length (E) 8.64m (28ft 4in), (G) 9.04m (29ft 8in); height (E) 2.28m (7ft 5½in), (G) 2.59m (8ft 6in)
**Weights:** empty (E) 1,900kg (4,189lb), (G) 2,667kg (5,880lb); loaded (E) 2,505kg (5,523lb), (G) 3,400kg (7,496lb)
**Performance:** maximum speed (E) 563km/h (350mph), (G) 640km/h (400mph); service ceiling (E) 10,500m (34,450ft), (G) 11,580m (38,000ft); range 700km (435 miles)
**Armament:** (E) one 20mm MG FF cannon firing through the propeller hub, two 7.9mm MG17 machine-guns firing through the propeller arc plus two MG FF in wings; (G) one 30mm MK 108 cannon, two MG131 above engine plus two MG 151 under wings

# MESSERSCHMITT Bf 110

Designed by Prof. Willy Messerschmitt as a long-range escort fighter. The prototype was powered by two DB 600 engines and made its maiden flight on 12 May 1936. Despite reaching a speed of 508km/h (316mph) this aircraft had poor maneouvrability and also heavy flight controls. The Bf 110 arrived in service in time for the 'Blitzkrieg' invasion of Poland, and was used successfully, mainly in the ground attack role. During the Battle of Britain losses of 110s were very high against superior RAF aircraft and the Luftwaffe was forced to use Bf 109s to escort the vulnerable Bf 110s which nevertheless continued to be produced in various models.

**Country of Origin:** Germany
**Type:** fighter
**Crew:** two–three
**Power Plant:** two 1,100hp Daimler Benz DB 601A-1 liquid-cooled inverted-vee-twelves
**Dimensions:** span 16.25m (53ft 3½in); length 12.07m (39ft 7¼in); height 4.13m (13ft 6½in); wing area 38.4m² (413sq ft)
**Weights:** empty 4,500kg (9,920lb); loaded 7,000kg (15,430lb)
**Performance:** maximum speed 562km/h (349mph); service ceiling 10,000m (32,810ft); range 1,100km (680 miles)
**Armament:** four forward firing 20mm MG FF cannon in nose plus one flexible 7.9mm MG15 machine-gun in rear cockpit

*A failure in the long-range fighter role during 1940, the Bf 110 proved an effective radar-equipped night fighter late in the war.*

Designed by Prof. Alexander Lippisch, the Komet was a point defence interceptor. Unpowered flight trials began with the Me 163V-1 in the spring of 1941, with the first powered flights made in August of that year. Its bi-propellant rocket motor gave it a phenomenal performance with a rate of climb of 5,000m/min (16,400ft/min) but also caused quite a few problems. Many Komets were lost in non-combat, ground accidents when the highly corrosive fuels leaked, combined and exploded. In combat their small size and extremely high speed made them very difficult targets for both the bombers' gunners and their escort fighters.

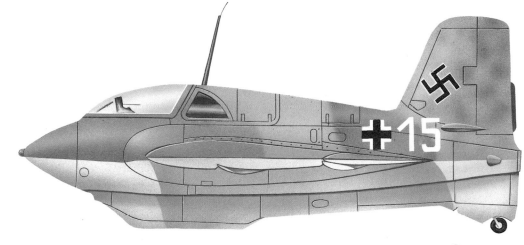

**Country of Origin:** Germany
**Type:** interceptor
**Crew:** one
**Power Plant:** one 1,700kg (3,750lb) thrust Walter HWK 509A-2 bi-propellant rocket motor, using hydrazine/methoanol (C-stoff) and concentrated hydrogen peroxide (T-stoff)
**Dimensions:** span 9.3m (30ft 7in); length 5.69m (18ft 8in); height 2.74m (9ft)
**Weights:** empty 1,901kg (4,191lb); loaded 4,101kg (9,042lb)
**Performance:** maximum speed 960km/h (596mph); service ceiling 16,500m (54,000ft); range 100km (62 miles); endurance (including climb) 8 minutes
**Armament:** two 30mm MK 108 cannon in wing roots

*A B-17 provides the backdrop for this Komet at the Imperial War Museum, Duxford.*

# MESSERSCHMITT Me 262A-1A

Had it not been for the insistence of Adolf Hitler that the Me 262 be developed mainly as a bomber, the Luftwaffe would probably have had, much earlier, an airplane with the potential to turn the tide of the air war raging in Europe's skies. Initial flight tests were conducted in April 1941, but using a single nose-mounted piston engine, with jet tests in July 1942. Frontline service did not start until autumn 1944.

**Country of Origin:** Germany
**Type:** interceptor fighter
**Crew:** one
**Power Plant:** two 900kg (1,984lb) thrust Junkers Jumo 004B-1, B-2 or B-3 single-shaft axial turbojets
**Dimensions:** span 12.5m (40ft 11½in); length 10.6m (34ft 9½in); height 3.8m (12ft 7in); wing area 21.7m² (234sq ft)
**Weights:** empty 4,000kg (8,820lb); loaded 7,045kg (15,500lb)
**Performance:** maximum speed 870km/h (540mph); service ceiling 11,450m (37,570ft); range 845km (525 miles)
**Armament:** four 30mm MK 108 cannon in nose, (bomber) two 500kg (1,000lb) bombs

*A Messerschmitt 262A V056 experimentally fitted with Lichtenstein SN-2 radar.*

Conceived to replace the Bf 110 in the long-range fighter role, the Me 210 was found during flight testing to have certain inherent instabilities. Of 1,000 aircraft ordered, only 352 were completed. Development work continued with the Me 310, a high altitude fighter bomber, but this project was itself curtailed in favour of the simpler Me 410, production of which started in late 1942.

**Country of Origin:** Germany
**Type:** fighter, attack, reconnaissance
**Crew:** two
**Power Plant:** two 1,750hp Daimler-Benz DB 603A liquid-cooled inverted-vee-twelves
**Dimensions:** span 16.35m (53ft 7½in); length 12.45m (40ft 10in); height 4.3m (14ft)
**Weights:** empty 6,150kg (13,560lb); loaded 10,650kg (23,483lb)
**Performance:** maximum speed 620km/h (385mph); service ceiling 10,000m (32,800ft); range 2,330km (1,447 miles)
**Armament:** normal versions, two fixed forward-firing 20mm MG151/20 and two 7.92mm MG17 in the nose, plus two 13mm MG131 in remotely-controlled barbettes on sides of fuselage

*A Messerschmitt Me 410A on display at the RAF Museum at Hendon in 1976.*

# MIKOYAN–GUREVICH MiG-3

Developed from the MiG-1, first of the Mikoyan-Gurevich design bureau aircraft, the MiG-3 differed from its predecessor in having an enclosed cockpit with improved rear vision, increased fuel capacity and increased dihedral on the outer wing panels. Due mainly to poor performance only some 2,100 MiG-1s and -3s were built.

**Country of Origin:** Soviet Union
**Type:** interceptor fighter
**Crew:** one
**Power Plant:** one 1,350hp Mikulin AM-35A liquid-cooled vee-twelve
**Dimensions:** span 10.3m (33ft 9½in); length 8.15m (26ft 9in); height 3.5m (11ft 6in); wing area 17.4m² (187.7sq ft)
**Weights:** empty 2,595kg (5,721lb); loaded 3,350kg (7,385lb)
**Performance:** maximum speed 640km/h (398mph); service ceiling 12,000m (39,370ft); range 1,250km (777 miles)
**Armament:** two 7.6mm ShKAS machine-guns plus one 13mm Beresin BS machine-gun in upper cowling; provision for 200kg (440lb) bombs or six 82mm RS82 rocket projectiles on underwing rails

*Even the starkness and long shadows of a Soviet winter afternoon cannot disguise the pleasing lines of this MiG-3.*

# MITSUBISHI A6M ZERO-SEN 'ZEKE' (A6M2 AND 5)

First flight of the A6M1 was made on 1 April 1939 powered by a 780hp Mitsubishi Zuisei. This engine was changed in favour of the more powerful Nakajima Sakae 12 when production started in 1940. At the time of Pearl Harbor the Japanese Navy had over 400 of the later A6M2s and M3s, which were far superior to the US Navy aircraft.

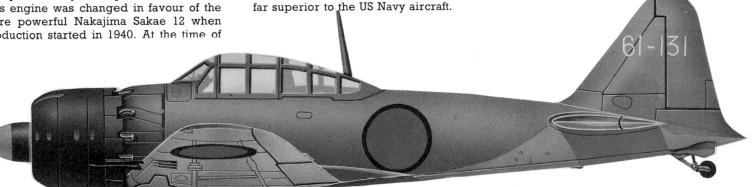

*An A6M5 captured by the Americans.*

**Country of Origin:** Japan
**Type:** naval fighter
**Crew:** one
**Power Plant:** (2) one 925hp Nakajima NK1C Sakae 12, (5) one 1,130hp Nakajima NK1F Sakae 21, both 14-cylinder two-row air-cooled radials
**Dimensions:** span (2) 12m (39ft 4½in), (5) 11m (36ft 1in); length 9.12m (29ft 11in); height (2) 2.92m (9ft 7in) (5) 2.95m (9ft 8in)
**Weights:** empty (2) 1,680kg (3,704lb), (5) 1,778kg (3,920lb); loaded (2) 2,410kg (5,313lb), (5) 2,744kg (6,050lb)
**Performance:** maximum speed (2) 509km/h (316mph) (5) 570km/h (354mph); service ceiling 10,300m (33,790ft), (5) 11,430m (37,500ft); drop tank range (2) 3,122km (1,940 miles), (5) 1,931km (1,200 miles)
**Armament:** (2) two 20mm Type 99 cannon in wings plus two 7.7mm Type 97 machine-guns in upper fuselage, (5) as with A6M2 but with one 7.7mm replaced by 12.7mm machine-gun. Both with wing racks for up to 60kg (132lb) of bombs

# NAKAJIMA Ki-43 HAYABUSA 'OSCAR' (Ki-43-III)

The Ki-43 was codenamed 'Oscar' by the Allies, and Hayabusa (Peregrin Falcon) by the Japanese Army. Designed by Dr. Hideo Itokawa and built in large numbers for the Japanese Imperial Army, the Ki-43 had excellent manoeuvrability but poor armament and armour.

**Country of Origin:** Japan
**Type:** interceptor fighter, fighter-bomber
**Crew:** one
**Power Plant:** one 1,250hp Nakajima Ha-112 Kasei 14-cylinder two-row air-cooled radial
**Dimensions:** span 10.83m (35ft 6½in); length 8.92m (29ft 3¼in); height 3.27m (10ft 8½in)
**Weights:** empty 1,990kg (4,387lb); loaded 2,850kg (6,283lb)
**Performance:** maximum speed 585km/h (363mph); service ceiling 11,735m (38,500ft); range 1,700km (1,060 miles) on internal fuel or 3,000km (1,864 miles) with two 170 litre (45 gallon) drop tanks
**Armament:** two 12.7mm Type 1 machine-guns in engine cowling with provision for 250kg (551lb) of bombs on underwing racks

*Nakajima Ki-43 'Oscar' fighters warming-up for take-off.*

40

# NORTH AMERICAN P-51 MUSTANG (P-51A AND D)

Arguably the best single-seat fighter of WWII, the Mustang was commissioned by the RAF from North American Aviation. NA's design team worked fast, and their airplane flew on 26 October 1940, a mere 117 days after the agreement. Initial RAF orders were for 620 aircraft, which started to enter service in November 1941, and with the USAAF in 1942. The RAF experimented with fitting a Merlin power plant and this later became the standard Mustang engine.

*An Allison-powered Mustang Mk I of the RAF's 2 Sqn in July 1942.*

**Country of Origin:** United States
**Type:** fighter, fighter-escort
**Crew:** one
**Power Plant:** (A) one 1,150hp Allison V-1710, (D) one 1,590hp Packard V-1650 licence-built Rolls-Royce Merlin, both liquid-cooled vee-twelve
**Dimensions:** span 11.29m (37ft $\frac{1}{2}$in); length 9.82m (32ft $2\frac{1}{2}$in); height (A) 3.72m (12ft 2in), (D) 4.1m (13ft 8in)
**Weights:** empty (A) 2,858kg (6,300lb), (D) 3,230kg (7,125lb); loaded (A) 3,901kg (8,600lb), (D) 5,260kg (11,600lb)
**Performance:** maximum speed (A) 628km/h (390mph), (D) 703km/h (437mph); service ceiling (A) 9,144m (30,000ft), (D) 12,770m (41,900ft); range (A) 724km (450 miles), (D) 1,528km (950 miles) on internal fuel or 2,092km (1,300 miles) with drop tanks
**Armament:** (A) four 0.5in machine-guns in the wings with provision for 227kg (500lb) of bombs, (D) six 0.5in Browning MG53-2 and provision for 454kg (1,000lb) of bombs

# NORTHROP P-61B BLACK WIDOW

Northrop's purpose-built night fighter, the Black Widow, first took to the air in prototype form as the XP-61 on 21 May 1942. It was designed to carry a new radar, the SCR-720A1, positioned in the nose. The aircraft's armament was located in a ventral fairing, and in a remotely controlled dorsal turret which was not fitted to most later models. The P-61A entered USAAF service in the South Pacific in May 1944 with the 18th fighter group. An unarmed photographic reconnaissance version, the F-15A, was produced after WWII.

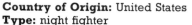

**Country of Origin:** United States
**Type:** night fighter
**Crew:** three
**Power Plant:** two 2,000hp Pratt & Whitney R-2800 Double Wasp 18-cylinder two-row air-cooled radial
**Dimensions:** span 20.12m (66ft); length 14.92m (48ft 11in); height 4.47m (14ft 8in)
**Weights:** empty 10,886kg (24,000lb); loaded 14,696kg (32,400lb)
**Performance:** maximum speed 590km/h (366mph); service ceiling 10,060m (33,000ft); range 805km (500 miles)
**Armament:** four forward-firing 20mm M-2 cannon in belly, four 0.5in machine-guns in remotely controlled dorsal turret

*A Northrop P-61A of the 422nd Night Fighter Sqn, USAAF, in August 1944.*

42

Following the results of early WWII air combat, Alexander Kartveli, Republic's chief designer, had to rethink rapidly his designs for a new fighter. In order to achieve the required range and performance, the highly powered Pratt & Whitney R-2800 Double Wasp engine was selected, resulting in the XP-47B prototype.

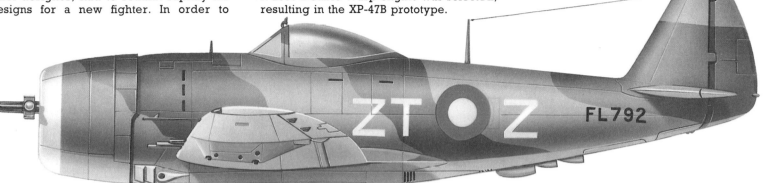

*A USAAF P-47C, 1943.*

**Country of Origin:** United States
**Type:** (B) fighter, (D) fighter-bomber
**Crew:** one
**Power Plant:** (B) one 2,000hp R-2800-21, (D) one 2,300hp R-2800-59, both Pratt & Whitney Double Wasp 18-cylinder two-row air-cooled radials
**Dimensions:** span 12.4m (40ft 9½in); length (B) 10.61m (34ft 10in), (D) 11m (36ft 1¼in); height (B) 3.86m (12ft 8in)
**Weights:** empty (B) 4,087kg (9,010lb), (D) 4,853kg (10,700lb); loaded (B) 5,760kg (12,700lb), (D) 8,800kg (19,400lb)
**Performance:** maximum speed (B) 663km/h (412mph), (D) 690km/h (428mph); service ceiling (B) 11,582m (38,000ft), (D) 13,100m (43,000ft); range (B) 925km (575 miles), (D) 1,600km (1,000 miles); range with drop tanks (D) 3,060km (1,900 miles)
**Armament:** eight 0.5in Colt-Browning M-2 machine-guns in the wings; (D) up to five external racks for either drop tanks, bombs or rockets with a maximum load of 1,134kg (2,500lb)

# SUPERMARINE SPITFIRE (Mk I AND IX)

The only Allied combat aircraft to remain in continuous production throughout WWII, and probably the most famous fighter of all time, it was designed by Reginald Mitchell who had gained design experience with the British Schneider Trophy racers. The Spitfire first flew on 5 March 1936 with RAF deliveries of Mk Is beginning in August 1938. 20,334 Spitfires were built, plus 2,556 of the navalized Seafire version.

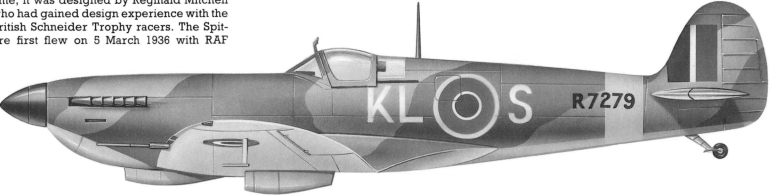

*A clipped-wing Spitfire Mk VB of 316 Sqn RAF photographed on 6 August 1943.*

**Country of Origin:** Great Britain
**Type:** fighter
**Crew:** one
**Power Plant:** (I) one 1,030hp Rolls-Royce Merlin II, (IX) one 1,660hp Rolls-Royce Merlin 61, both liquid-cooled vee-twelve
**Dimensions:** span 11.23m (36ft 10in), (clipped wing) 9.8m (32ft 2in); length (I) 9.12m (29ft 11in), (IX) 9.54m (31ft 3½in); height 3.48m (11ft 5in)
**Weights:** empty (I) 2,182kg (4,810lb), (IX) 2,545kg (5,610kg); loaded (I) 2,624kg (5,784lb), (IX) 4,310kg (9,500lb)
**Performance:** maximum speed (I) 580km/h (360mph), (IX) 657km/h (408mph); service ceiling 10,300m (33,800ft); range (I) 636km (395 miles), (IX) 700km (434 miles)
**Armament:** (I) eight 0.303in Browning machine-guns in the wings, (IB) two 20mm Hispano cannon plus four 0.303in Brownings, (IXA) eight 0.303in Brownings, (XIB) two 20mm and four Brownings, (XIC) either plus provision for 113kg (250lb) bombs

The Vought V-166B's first flight was on 29 May 1940 and it was the first US warplane to fly faster then 644km/h (400mph). The Corsair's unusual inverted gull-wing was designed to give a reasonable ground clearance to the large-diameter propeller without the need for excessively long undercarriage legs.

**Country of Origin:** United States
**Type:** naval fighter
**Crew:** one
**Power Plant:** one 2,000hp Pratt & Whitney R-2800-8 Double Wasp 18-cylinder two-row air-cooled radial
**Dimensions:** span 12.5m (41ft); length 10.2m (33ft 4in); height 4.6m (15ft 1in); wing area 29.2m² (314sq ft)
**Weights:** empty 3,990kg (8,800lb); loaded 6,350kg (14,000lb)
**Performance:** maximum speed 602km/h (374mph); service ceiling 10,360m (34,000ft); range 1,810km (1,125 miles)
**Armament:** four or six 0.5in machine-guns in wings

*This photograph of an F4U shows the aircraft's inverted gull-wing to good effect.*

# YAKOVLEV YAK-9 (D AND P)

Development of the Yak-7 led to the Yak-7DI, a long-range version differing from the original in the use of light alloys in its construction. Production began in autumn 1942 as the Yak-9: development continued and new marks were produced – the Yak-9B bomber, the 9T and K anti-tank and the 9D for long range, and the very long-range 9DD.

*A photograph of a Yugoslav Air Force Yak 9 taken in Italy in 1946.*

**Country of Origin:** Soviet Union
**Type:** fighter
**Crew:** one
**Power Plant:** (D) one 1,260hp Klimov VK-105PF, (P) one 1,650hp VK-107A, both liquid-cooled vee-twelve
**Dimensions:** span 10m (32ft 9½in); length (D) 8.54m (28ft ½in), (P) 8.7m (28ft 6½in); height 2.44m (8ft)
**Weights:** empty (D) 2,750kg (6,063lb), (P) 2,313kg (5,100lb); loaded (D) 3,200kg (7,055lb), (P) 3,170kg (6,988lb)
**Performance:** maximum speed (D) 578km/h (359mph), (P) 670km/h (416mph); service ceiling 10,500m (34,500ft); range (D) 1,350km (840 miles), (P) 890km (550 miles)
**Armament:** one 20mm ShVAK cannon firing through the propeller hub, two 12.7mm Beresin in engine cowling firing through the propeller arc, provision for two 100kg (220lb) bombs